Lerner **SPORTS**

SANDY KOUFAX
LEFTY LEGEND

PERCY LEED

LERNER PUBLICATIONS ◆ MINNEAPOLIS

Lerner Publications Company
An imprint of Lerner Publishing Group, Inc.
241 First Avenue North
Minneapolis, MN 55401 USA

For reading levels and more information, look up this title at www.lernerbooks.com.

Main body text set in Myriad Pro Semibold.
Typeface provided by Adobe.

Editor: Alison Lorenz **Designer:** Susan Fienhage
Lerner team: Sue Marquis

Library of Congress Cataloging-in-Publication Data

Names: Leed, Percy, 1968– author.
Title: Sandy Koufax : lefty legend / Percy Leed.
Description: Minneapolis : Lerner Publications, 2021 | Series: Epic sports bios (Lerner sports) | Includes bibliographical references and index. | Audience: Ages 7–11 | Audience: Grades 4–6 | Summary: "Sandy Koufax went from dreaming of playing in the NBA to pitching perfect games for the Los Angeles Dodgers. Learn how the left-handed Koufax honed his throwing arm, brought the Dodgers a World Series, and more"— Provided by publisher.
Identifiers: LCCN 2019053398 (print) | LCCN 2019053399 (ebook) | ISBN 9781728414690 (library binding) | ISBN 9781728414751 (paperback) | ISBN 9781728414768 (ebook)
Subjects: LCSH: Koufax, Sandy, 1935– —Juvenile literature. | Baseball players—United States—Biography—Juvenile literature. | Los Angeles Dodgers (Baseball team)—Biography—Juvenile literature.
Classification: LCC GV865.K67 L45 2021 (print) | LCC GV865.K67 (ebook) | DDC 796.357092 [B]—dc23

LC record available at https://lccn.loc.gov/2019053398
LC ebook record available at https://lccn.loc.gov/2019053399

Manufactured in the United States of America
1-48650-49073-3/4/2020

CONTENTS

WORLD SERIES SHUTOUT

Los Angeles Dodgers pitcher Sandy Koufax walked to the mound for Game 7 of the 1965 World Series against the Minnesota Twins. Koufax was the best pitcher in the big leagues. But he was pitching on little rest, and arthritis, a painful joint condition, troubled his left elbow. Baseball fans knew that Koufax could shut down any lineup. But could he do it in this game?

Sandy Koufax hurls a pitch during the 1965 World Series.

FACTS AT A GLANCE

Date of birth: December 30, 1935

Position: pitcher

League: Major League Baseball

Professional highlights: pitched a record-tying 18 strikeouts in a single game in 1959; won the National League (NL) Most Valuable Player (MVP) Award, World Series MVP Award, and Cy Young Award in 1963; retired early due to arthritis in his left arm

Personal highlights: missed Game 1 of the 1965 World Series to observe Yom Kippur; studied to become an architect; became the youngest person inducted into baseball's Hall of Fame at the age of 36

Koufax got the Twins' first two batters out. But he walked the next two. Dodgers manager Walter Alston prepared to pull his star pitcher out of the game.

Koufax, though, had other plans. After three shutout innings, the Dodgers pulled into a 2–0 lead in the fourth. Koufax decided that two runs would be enough. Inning after inning passed with no change to the score.

Koufax earned his second series MVP award for shutting out the Twins.

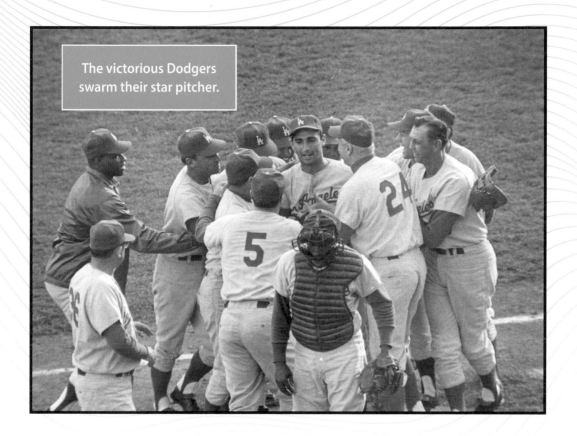

The victorious Dodgers swarm their star pitcher.

Finally, it was the bottom of the ninth. Koufax needed just three more outs to give the Dodgers the World Series. The Twins' Tony Oliva grounded out. Harmon Killebrew hit a single, but Koufax struck out Earl Battey. One more out and the game was over. Bob Allison was down to his last strike.

Koufax delivered his last pitch of the day, a blazing fastball. Allison took a mighty swing—and missed. Just like that, Koufax had made the Dodgers World Series champions.

BROOKLYN BOY

Sanford (Sandy) Braun was born in Brooklyn, New York, on December 30, 1935. His family lived near other Jewish families in a middle-class neighborhood.

When Sandy was three, his father divorced his mother. Sandy and his mother moved in with her parents. While his mother worked, Sandy spent time with his grandparents. Sandy's grandfather was a devoted Jew. He instilled a sense of cultural pride in his grandson.

Koufax at home with his parents, Evelyn and Irving Koufax.

At an early age, Sandy showed he was an athlete. He loved any kind of sport. He spent hours playing baseball in the streets of Brooklyn. He watched the Brooklyn Dodgers play at the nearby Ebbets Field.

When Sandy was nine, his mother married Irving Koufax. Sandy took his new father's last name, and the two quickly grew close. After several family moves, Sandy began to spend time at the Jewish Community House in Bensonhurst, a Brooklyn neighborhood. There he played basketball, swam, and lifted weights. Wherever his family was, Sandy played every sport he could.

A MAN OF FAITH

Game 1 of the 1965 World Series fell on Yom Kippur, the holiest of Jewish holidays. Though he was the obvious choice to start, Koufax put his faith first and decided not to pitch the game.

The New York Knicks play the Syracuse Nationals in 1951.

In high school, Sandy was a star basketball player. When a coaches' strike shut down the athletics program at his school, Sandy brought his skills back to the Jewish Community House. He led their basketball team to a championship. "This guy was a world-class athlete at the age of seventeen," said their director of athletics.

In his senior year, Sandy had the chance to play against some players from the New York Knicks basketball team. The pro players were impressed. Sandy looked as if he had a future as a pro athlete. But nobody would have guessed that he would play baseball.

BOUND FOR BASEBALL

Sandy didn't play high school baseball until his senior year. The manager of a local team, the Parkviews, asked Sandy to play for them. He wanted to try the strong lefty as a pitcher.

Sandy had a blazing fastball. He sometimes threw wildly. But when he was on, he was devastating. He threw a no-hitter in one of his first games for the Parkviews and quickly became the team's best pitcher. Before long, major-league scouts were watching him.

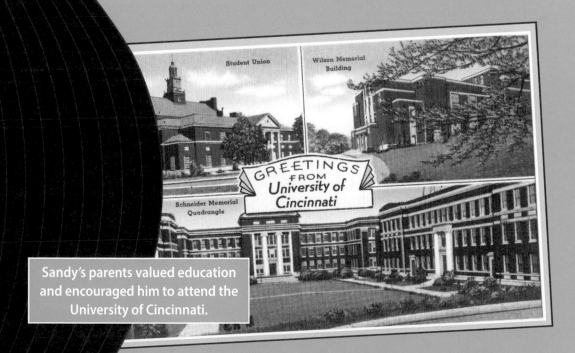

Sandy's parents valued education and encouraged him to attend the University of Cincinnati.

But Sandy's baseball career would have to wait. He had decided to attend the University of Cincinnati in Ohio in the fall. There he would play basketball and pursue his dream of becoming an architect.

At Cincinnati, first-year players were on a different basketball team than players in the upper classes. Sandy performed well for the freshmen team. But he dreamed of competing with the older players. Then he learned that players on the university's baseball team were allowed to compete with the varsity team as freshmen.

LOOKING FOR LEFTIES

Major-league teams are always interested in a left-handed pitcher who can throw hard. Because these pitchers are so rare, batters often have a harder time hitting their pitches.

Koufax in his college baseball uniform in 1954

He asked his coach, Ed Jucker, if he could try out to pitch for the baseball team on their spring break trip.

Koufax gathered in the gym with other players hoping to earn a spot on the trip. When it was his turn, he fired his hardest fastball. The catcher caught it, and then he stood up and left. It hurt too much to catch any more of Koufax's pitches. "It's like a revelation to see someone throw the ball that fast," Jucker said.

Jucker wasted little time getting Koufax into a game. Koufax's amazing fastball and good curveball attracted a lot of attention from other teams. Hitters feared him. Scouts from the major leagues began to notice.

One scout came from the Brooklyn Dodgers. He was impressed with Koufax's powerful arm and thought coaches could work with him to improve his control. The Dodgers offered him a big contract.

Koufax signed with the Brooklyn Dodgers when he was just 18 years old.

Koufax (*second row, third from left*) poses with the rest of the Brooklyn Dodgers.

Koufax spoke with his father. They decided that he could attend classes during the off-season, so he accepted the offer. In less than a year, Koufax had gone from a college basketball player to a pro pitcher for the Brooklyn Dodgers.

STUCK IN THE MAJORS

With the Dodgers, Koufax trained harder than he ever had. Coaches worked with him to control his pitches. But Alston, the team's manager, wasn't ready to play him against a major-league team.

Koufax was in a tough situation. At the time, players who signed with bonuses as high as his couldn't be sent to the minors. Stuck in the majors, he wasn't good enough

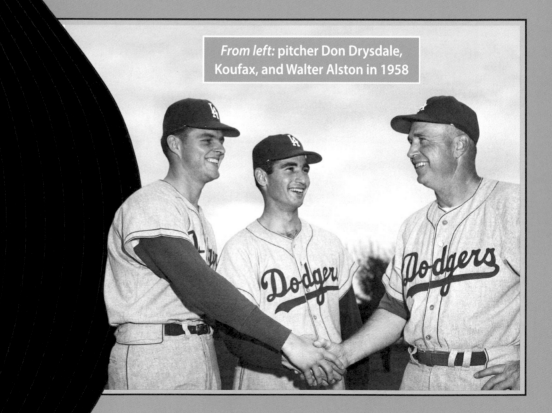

From left: pitcher Don Drysdale, Koufax, and Walter Alston in 1958

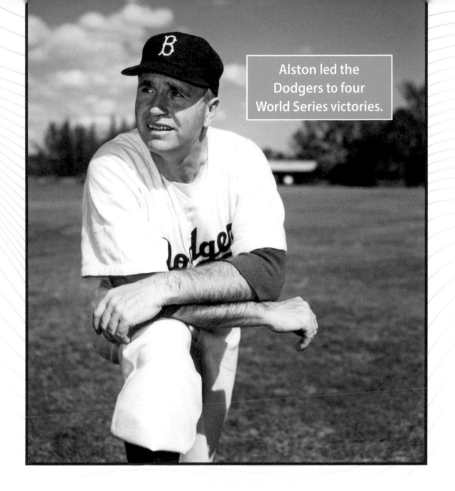

Alston led the Dodgers to four World Series victories.

to put into a close game, and he couldn't get better without more chances to pitch. Finally, Alston gave him a chance. In his second career start, Koufax pitched an incredible 14 strikeouts. It was the highest total for any NL pitcher in the 1955 season. Starting again a week later, he struck out six Pittsburgh Pirates, and the Dodgers won in a shutout. But when the Dodgers won the World Series later that season, Koufax was on the bench again.

The following season, fans and reporters began to pressure Alston to give Koufax more playing time. Alston refused. Koufax played more than he had in his first season. But his performance was worse, and his confidence suffered.

At the start of his third season, Koufax had just 30 days before the Dodgers would send him to the minor leagues. He had spent the off-season training hard. He was ready to prove himself.

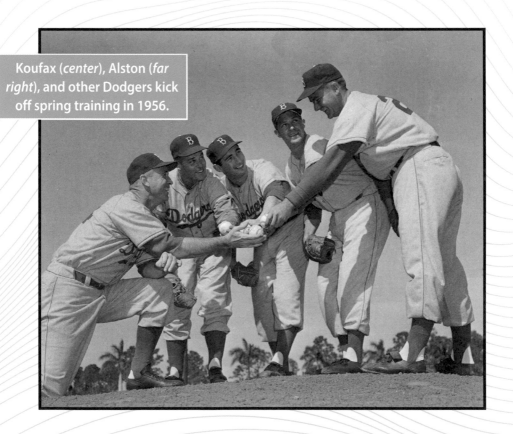

Koufax (*center*), Alston (*far right*), and other Dodgers kick off spring training in 1956.

Koufax's teammates rushed to shake his hand after the pitcher struck out 14 Cincinnati Redlegs in 1955.

Alston decided to give him one last shot. Koufax was pitching for his future when he took the mound at Wrigley Field to face the Chicago Cubs. He struck out 13 Cubs and helped the Dodgers to a 3–2 victory. Alston didn't send Koufax to the minor leagues. He gave him a spot in the starting rotation.

In fewer than 50 innings, Koufax pitched 59 strikeouts, more than any other NL pitcher at that point in the season. Koufax was pitching better and better, and he had the stats to prove it.

The move to Los Angeles began a new phase in Koufax's career.

AN EARLY END

In 1958, the Brooklyn Dodgers moved to California and became the Los Angeles Dodgers. Koufax began his first season there pitching well. But it seemed that just when things started to go his way, he faced a new setback.

Early in the season, an ankle injury threw Koufax off his game. He had earned a reputation: he was either spectacular or awful. Fans wondered if Alston had made

Koufax winds up a pitch in 1958.

Koufax pitched four no-hitters, the last in 1965.

the right choice in keeping him. For once, Alston was Koufax's defender. "You can't give up on him," he said.

Koufax showed he could still pitch an amazing game. In 1959, he tied the record for most strikeouts in a single game, with 18 against the San Francisco Giants. But things didn't finally click until the spring before Koufax's seventh season, when a backup catcher suggested he not try to throw so hard. When Koufax relaxed, everything came together. His pitches were as fast as ever, and his control became spot-on.

In 1961, Koufax broke the NL record for most strikeouts in a season—a record that had stood for over 50 years—with 269. The following year he tied his single-game strikeout record again. Of the 144 pitches he threw that day, 96 were strikes. "I lost track of how many strikeouts I had today," he told reporters.

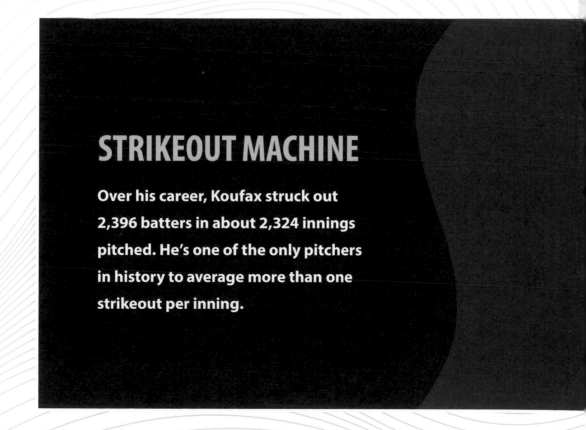

STRIKEOUT MACHINE

Over his career, Koufax struck out 2,396 batters in about 2,324 innings pitched. He's one of the only pitchers in history to average more than one strikeout per inning.

The 1963 season was another eventful one for Koufax. He helped bring the Dodgers another World Series. He won the NL MVP Award, the World Series MVP Award, and the Cy Young Award for his incredible pitching.

Koufax throws a pitch during the 1963 World Series.

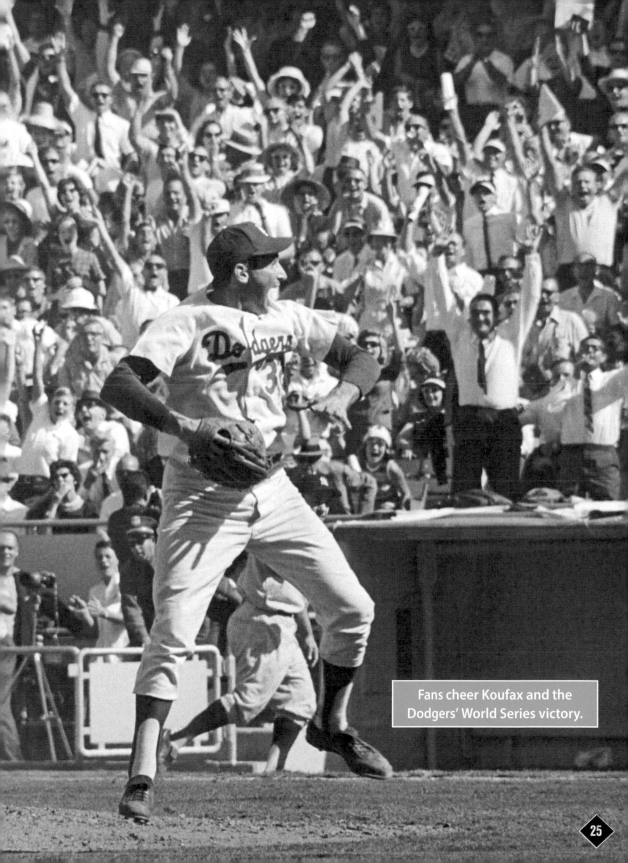

Fans cheer Koufax and the Dodgers' World Series victory.

But he also kept racking up the injuries that would end his career early. In 1962, Koufax nearly needed his finger amputated when it lost blood flow. Within two years, he found he could not straighten his left arm. Doctors diagnosed him with arthritis.

Koufax still had one World Series left in him. He clinched the 1965 win after striking out a record 382 batters over the season. But the following year was Koufax's last in pro baseball. Though he was just 30 years old, the arthritis in his pitching arm had become too painful. "I've got a lot of years to live after baseball," he said. "I don't regret one minute of the last twelve years, but I think I would regret one year that was too many."

Koufax ices his pitching arm after a game in 1965.

Koufax interviews Leo Durocher, manager of the Chicago Cubs, in 1967.

For years, Koufax stuck around the world of baseball. He got a job on the TV network NBC discussing games. At the age of 36, he became the youngest person ever inducted into baseball's Hall of Fame. He spent more than a decade with the Dodgers as a minor-league pitching coach.

Though Koufax is no longer involved in baseball, fans can't help but wonder what might have been. Koufax retired at an age when most players are hitting their peaks. But fans are grateful for the years Koufax gave to the sport. His years of amazing pitching are unmatched in baseball history.

SELECTED CAREER STATISTICS

Strikeouts Per Season

Year	Innings Pitched	Strikeouts
1955	41	30
1956	58	30
1957	104	122
1958	158	131
1959	153	173
1960	175	197
1961	255	269
1962	184	216
1963	311	306
1964	223	223
1965	335	382
1966	323	317

GLOSSARY

curveball: a pitch that curves as it approaches the batter

fastball: a pitch thrown at full speed

ground out: when a batter hits a ball on the ground to a fielder who throws it to or steps on first base

no-hitter: a game in which a pitcher allows the other team no base hits

off-season: the time a sports team does not play

pro: an activity for money

scout: someone who judges the talent of potential players

shutout: a game in which one side fails to score

strikeout: an out in baseball after a batter gets three strikes

SOURCE NOTES

10   Jane Leavy, *Sandy Koufax: A Lefty's Legacy* (New York: HarperCollins, 2002), 188.

13   Edward Gruver, *Koufax* (Dallas: Taylor, 2000), 32.

22   Gruver, 122.

23   Gruver, 137.

26   Gruver, 211–212.

FURTHER INFORMATION

Baseball Reference: Sandy Koufax
https://www.baseball-reference.com/players/k/koufasa01.shtml

Fishman, Jon M. *Baseball's G.O.A.T.: Babe Ruth, Mike Trout, and More.* Minneapolis: Lerner Publications, 2020.

Frederickson, Kevin. *Major League Baseball.* Minnetonka, MN: Kaleidoscope, 2019.

Major League Baseball
https://www.mlb.com/

National Baseball Hall of Fame: Sandy Koufax
https://baseballhall.org/hall-of-famers/koufax-sandy

Rajczak, Michael. *The Greatest Baseball Players of All Time.* New York: Gareth Stevens, 2020.

INDEX

PHOTO ACKNOWLEDGMENTS

Image credits: Bettmann/Getty Images, pp. 4, 7, 10, 13, 14, 15, 16, 17, 18, 22, 24, 25, 26, 27; Andrey_PopovShutterstock.com, pp. 5, 28; Focus on Sport/Getty Images, p. 6; Charles Hoff/New York Daily News Archive/Getty Images, pp. 8, 19; Boston Public Library/flickr (CC BY 2.0), p. 11; Louis Requena/Major League Baseball/Getty Images, pp. 20, 21. Design element throughout: saicle/iStock/Getty Images.

Cover: Bettmann/Getty Images.